Jesus of Walmart

Jesus of Walmart

Poems

Richard Broderick

NØY Books™

The New York Quarterly Foundation, Inc.
New York, New York

NYQ Books™ is an imprint of The New York Quarterly Foundation, Inc.

The New York Quarterly Foundation, Inc.
P. O. Box 2015
Old Chelsea Station
New York, NY 10113

www.nyq.org

First Edition

Set in New Baskerville

Layout by Raymond P. Hammond

Cover Design by Raymond P. Hammond

Cover Art by Svetlana Rumak | www.rumak.net

Author Photo by Petronella J. Ytsma | www.petronellaytsma.com

Library of Congress Control Number: 2016930016

ISBN: 978-1-63045-019-9

Jesus of Walmart

Contents

V.

Jesus of Walmart

What's in a Name?

Five syllables. That's all.
Barely a breath and a-half.
That's all.

A blur at the edge of a picture frame.
A face reflected in a storefront window.
A word written backward in a looking glass.

Not the flame, just the mantle.
Another's hand lit the wick.
Another's breath blows out the light.

Hear that singing in the distance?
See those lanterns flickering in the dark?
Pilgrims are already dancing down the road.
Hurry now. Maybe you can catch them!

I.

The Dogs Are Barking in the Neighborhood Tonight

From yard to yard they call each other,
"I hear you!" They scratch the gate,
whimper and moan at the street lamp's artificial moon.
In the shadows they pace and scratch,
crazed by a wildness they don't understand,
leaping fences in their dreams, tails wagging
stiffly when they collide.
They want to chase the wolf
inside themselves down the street.
They want to grow their fangs and claws.
They want their legs to lengthen and their paws
to widen into the forest's loping gait.
The dogs are barking in the neighborhood tonight.
Slow down, you dogs! Slow down,
you wolves! I am lonely too!

All Present And Accounted For

Earth is the heaven of animals.
It is only on earth they are fully
present and no where else. (Even
in your dreams, the wolf and
the snake are no more than shadows
of your projection.) No brown bear

ever waded the fall run, catching
salmon, but wishing he were
someplace else. No milk cow
plans for the future or dreams
of changing places with the sleek
Jersey on the cover of this month's

Dairy Digest. Dogs do not fall
into a brown study, cats have
no second thoughts, the honey-
bee gives it full attention
to the hive or the flower.
Horse and cattle may be driven

to distraction by biting flies
(themselves a model of insistent
presence), but in doing so they
give themselves to madness
without stint. That goat you saw
while out driving in the country

wasn't really sullen; that was some
feeling of your own you'd rather
leave behind standing on a hillside
glaring at the road. Yes,
you have seen apes and lions
looking bored, but that was

at the zoo, where they were trapped
in man-made enclosures, boxes
like the ones you've always lived in.
So maybe the soul—the soul you're
not sure animals even possess—
maybe that's the name you give

to the part of yourself you have
no power to withhold. And maybe
heaven, maybe that's where you
hope someday to be fully present,
the garden where we'll all be
reborn into our animal selves.

Hand-Me-Downs

A kid with two older brothers—
of course you hardly wore
anything but hand-me-downs.
But did you mind? Not really.

Sure the fit might be a little off,
cuffs and collars frayed some,
and shoes loose enough
to chafe your heel.
Even so those clothes felt
tailored-made for a slightly older
version of you, the skin you were
going to grow up and fill out,
with the elbow room
already broken in,
plenty of space for your knees
and shoulders to expand,
the soles of the shoes and sneakers
shaped by miles hiked,
you could almost swear,
in your name.

And the buttonholes!
Stiffness lost, they were
soft and eager to receive
the plastic hosts you pushed
into the their open mouths,
making it so much easier
to achieve your never-changing goal—
get buttoned up as
quick as possible

and get on your way.

Boys Fishing

All the way across the pond
I hear them curse their tackle,
their tangled reels,
watch as they snag lures
in low-hanging branches,
while below, their
blurred reflections
rock calmly on the surface.

Who are these quiet spirits
rising to join them after
a long swim in the depths?
Sitting on the grass,
I glimpse my own reflection,
finding no name for estrangement,
no memory of when
my edgy shore-bound "I"
divided from the "me"
swimming peacefully
in motherly brown water.

Having freed his line,
one of the boys casts
across his own image,
calls to his friend and cackles.
I watch as he cranks
and cranks the reel,
trying to tow his
own shadow back to land.

The Barges

I give thanks every time
I spot one rounding
a slow bend in the river
and coming into view
with all the plodding dignity
of a big draft animal
plowing a wake
down the middle
of a field.
I love the sight of them,
the smell of them,
the voices of the deck hands
bouncing off the water
and landing loud and clear
even up here on
the far shore.

Sometimes,
they ride low, the barges,
borne down by loads
of gravel or sand
or jet-black cones
of coal hauled
all the way home
from the Carboniferous.
Other times they ride
high, burdened
by nothing weightier
than sunlight,
the echo of voices
and the slight freight
of a heart
buoyed by happiness.

For Local Poets Everywhere

To you the mystery of the missing signpost,
directions to the swimming hole,
the best place to pick blackberries (or raspberries
in season) and the quickest way
to jumpstart the old car.

And to you the now nearly forgotten name
of the family who lived in the house over there, the one
that just sold again for the second time this year,
and the old lady with the German accent who walked
her blind dog in every kind of weather,
both of them limping from hip dysplasia.

And to you the drama that took place
in front of the upstairs window every evening
and what things looked like
before the freeway came through
and the bottling plant shut down
and the annual company picnic called it a day.

And to you the taste of milk delivered
to the front door, the cream forcing open
the caps on winter mornings,
the melancholy gaze of the drunk who lived
with his parents and the ambulance that came
one rainy morning and took him away.

And to you the sound of your mother's voice
across the years, thinner, higher,
then falling silent, and of the clatter
over dinner next door, arguments across
the back fence, the whine of mosquitoes
on close nights, and dogs barking
as the mailman made his way down the street.

And to you the sight of kids running free
on sunny days, lightning bugs in a jar,
arguments about how far away the stars were
or the rules to made-up games, when whoever won today
might win the next and you could leave off
when it got too dark to see anymore because you
knew someone else was bound to come along
tomorrow and finish whatever you started.

Photograph of The Students in the One-Room
Finnish Schoolhouse, Esko, Minnesota, 1914

So they will not be forgotten—
so we will not forget them—
the names are written in chalk
that no one can erase
on the blackboard behind the children
who gather in front of their teacher,
a young woman not much older
than her students—Ida, Eddie,
Joseph, and Yalmer Juntunen,
Silvia Kangas, the Polo kids,
Olga, Charles, and Hilda,
two dozen more. At 12:26 p.m.,
according to the clock on the wall,
out of the fresh-faced light of 1914,
the children stare with questioning
looks: Do we remember?
Who grew up to become a drunkard,
who fell through the ice and drowned
the winter of 1927, who'd already lost
her mother and father to the Spanish Flu,
which pair, the girl taller here than
her future husband, married and had
four children, three of whom survived,
who hanged himself near the bog,
who had sixteen great-grandchildren,
whose family lost its farm and moved
to the city, and who of these ended up
a wrinkled 104-year-old woman
in a Lutheran nursing home,
dozing most of the day,
unsure even what year it is,
but still able to recall, as though it were
yesterday, the scent of damp wool
drying by the woodstove,

long rainy afternoons sitting
at her desk, inkstained fingers,
the shuffling feet of children
lining up to be photographed,
the names of each
and every schoolmate.

My Grandfather at Rest

I close my eyes on a summer afternoon,
and see my grandfather, asleep in his armchair,
there in the old Brooklyn side-by-side.
The upholstery worn smooth behind his head,
his forearms angle over the armrests
like oars of a boat drifting with the current.

He's still wearing his glasses, *The Daily News*
draped across his belly, the piping on his long-sleeve
undershirt frayed, his toothless mouth
open slightly, a soft hole collapsing
every time he breathes. I can even see
the stump of his ring-finger where
a dockyard accident severed the bone—
the same stump he liked to use to scare us kids
when he was awake, grabbing our elbows
in what he called "The Devil's Handshake."

How many ships did this old man have to unload,
how many mornings huddle in a Pea Coat
waiting for his name to be called, how many nights
come home too tired to eat in order
to earn this 30 minutes of deathlike sleep?
On the table beside him, a half-finished glass
of Rheingold fizzes in the quiet summer air.
Outside, I hear my cousins argue their way
through a game of kick-the-can in the driveway
separating his house from my Uncle John's.

Careful now. I must not wake him.

The Boxing Lesson

"Keep it light, boys. Keep it light,"
my father would shout from the sidelines,
meaning light on our feet, dancing and circling,
never coming in direct at your opponent,
like that time my youngest brother
walked right into my straight-armed left
and knocked himself flat.

It was as if his sons were figures
in a myth whose feet might take root
the instant we stopped moving,
a suit of chainmail bark creeping up
over our thighs and trunks, freezing
us in place so we'd end up reeling
punch drunk before the fists of any breeze.

If, as he taught us, I look for movement
out of the corner of my eye
("The punch you don't see coming
is the one you've got to watch for"),
I can glimpse him out there in the blue arena,
dancing and circling, always moving,
as he boxes Death himself,
snapping back the hooded head
with a crisp one-two.

Swimming Laps

I swim an hour as if to chase the boy
I was, drowning, drowned,

beneath the closing waters
of the past, the boy who splashed

all day down by the beach, who could
hold his breath until his father,

watching, reached the point of panic.
Now, breathless, my father lies

at depths beyond the gasp of fear,
while in the pool, just past a mile

earned lap by lap, I seem to slip
inside another skin in which

the boy I was and the man I am
swim toward each other, breathing

easily now, side-by-side, afloat
in memory, our native element.

Draft

The dearly dead? Barely departed.
    You feel them even now
        gathering ground.

This early on a winter night,
    the sky's not dark enough yet
        to spark the Evening Star into life.

But you? You're nothing
    but a shadow yourself,
        a silhouette glimpsed

through a dimly lit window
    wrapping a scarf
        around your neck

not because of any chill
    but against the unmistakable draft
        that appears as if

out of nowhere every time
    the door between this world
        and the next

opens wide and sings.

II.

After Reading The Unabomber Manifesto

I know the kind of hut he hid out in,
the heaps of paper yellowing
like rotten snow beneath freckled
windows, the pages of magazines
and books rustled by the wind's
forefinger, up a rocky draw
where the pine boughs swish
like beaded curtains, the silence outside
a physical presence, the air at noon
baking in the reflected heat
of black scree sprawling downslope,
a solitary Camp Jay preening and
screeching on a lower branch,
and always the dryness, cracking
the mouth from the inside out,
tongue whiskery, the lips looking branded
as if they'd held smoldering words too long.
And no relief in the distances,
no dust of someone approaching
with a cry of love, no news
of a reprieve. In that solitude, he
came at last to see the way they
put him together, intricate mechanism
hair-triggered to explode like a fireweed
releasing its seed to the flames.
But there was no fire here, nothing
but the slow combustion of being
alone all the time, day and night.
And so, from the parts of himself,
he re-configured his packages,
wrapped in plain brown paper to signify
simplicity, and dispatched them
to places beyond the thunder,
messages from a new Thoreau.

At the Auto Junkyard

These engines purr inside the Cave of Shadows now,
the ideal world where rust and pitted windshields
are never known, where twisted frames and faded
paint jobs and roof tops dinked by hail
have no dominion beneath a sun that restores
the manmade products of our dreams
to mint-condition. Here is mother's car
and brother's classy chassis and the old man's
brute V-8, all 200 horses run off into the ether,
the missing engine block beneath the missing hood
as mysterious as a fist raised in anger, then withdrawn.
And here the eldest daughter's ride to night school,
the cushions disemboweled like her doomed ambition.
And here, those Sundays at the lake,
those trips out West, those sad processions
to nursing homes and graves,
the letting go and moving on, the amnesia
of America's good-intentions, our vain resolutions
to keep it clean, fix it up, stick to the dealer's
maintenance schedule: all here, in a tangle
of steel and rubber and fragments of tinted plastic.
Propped up on tire rims, this fleet of ghost cars
ferries our dead across the brackish river,
those who fell from the sky, those who leaped
from burning buildings, one black body
for every bent steering wheel, lipless smiles
below lidless eyes that stare straight ahead
through shattered glass, past the ranks of ruined cars,
the sagging cyclone fence, the weedy verge,
the litter of abandoned lives.

Hardly Paradise

Returning to the garden we were struck
by how much smaller it was than we remembered.
Could the olive tree that seemed to touch
the heavens themselves and whose lowest branch
we could not reach even when we stretched on tiptoes
really be this unprepossessing growth not much taller
than a shrub in the center of a little clearing?

Could the mountain that once took us half a day
to climb and whose summit commanded
a sweeping view of the countryside for miles around
prove to be nothing more than this hillock
looking out over a few acres of wooded parkland
like those we've wandered through countless times?

Could the four rivers that water the garden
and that in memory sweep along faster
than the swiftest horse, the silhouette of their far banks
barely visible in the distance, truly be this quartet
of pleasant but by no means impressive streams
whose deepest pools barely reach our ankles now
and whose width we can cross dry shod
by the end of summer?

It's true, the caretaker who stayed behind to keep
an eye on things when we were asked to leave
has done a wonderful job—what an angel!
Everything has been maintained exactly as it was
the day we departed, like the room of a child
whose parents cannot accept his death.

But, really, we must admit now
that we regret, a little, all the fighting and the killing,
the young men maimed in body and spirit
during our great military campaigns,

the multitude of failed marriages, the neglected children,
the drinking and lynching and midnight barn burnings,
the insomnia and depression, the lying and infidelity,
the years of therapy, the lack of love,
the kind word that might have made all the difference
if only we'd spoken it, the bitterness
of broken promises, the years spent nursing grudges,

the lifetime of happiness foregone in the name
of that day when we would finally reclaim
our birthright, recapture our homeland
and return in triumph to dwell once more
in a garden that, it so happens, is a nice enough spot
but hardly paradise.

This Endless Night

title of a Palestinian lullaby
from the CD Lullabies from the Axis of Evil

This endless night,
this endless night,
I hear you cry
but cannot see you.
Jackals in the olive grove,
wolves at the checkpoints,
and in a suitcase
waiting by the door,
what's left of baba's bones.

Who built this house
on the bridge of life?
How long will it stand
if we never return?
Each dawn is swallowed
by a hissing flare.
Water from our well flushes
the keepers' drains.

This endless night,
this endless night,
how can I soothe you
when I myself am afraid?
What can I leave you,
except eyes that refuse
to adjust to darkness,
except a dream of daylight
finally breaking
on our side of the sky?

North of San Diego

Westward the sun, which, in progressing so,
carves deep shadows into hillside arroyos
and raises to a threadbare glow the dry grasses
that grow beside highways that ignore
the country's natural roll, hurrying north and south
across valleys woven into the shape of baskets
once used to gather nuts and seeds and wild grains.
Last year, this county burned for weeks, suburban
cul-de-sacs going up in flames like chaparral
and eucalyptus trees. But whatever has happened
on this coast, whether in history or before,
is buried now beneath 12-lanes of concrete whose
cloverleaf exchanges turn back upon themselves
like the thoughts of a mind so cut off from the world
they have no place else to go. And now, with the sun
dissolving into the horizon, the ocean seems less to heave
than loom, rising from its bed like the trapdoor
to some bright room where the local gods of rivers
and fields, fertility and childbirth have fled,
and are fleeing still, like deer before a firestorm.

Imperial Lexicon

Theoretically,
death is not a personal experience.
Historically,
there's no comparison
between us and the Mongols.
Scripturally speaking,
there was Cain and Abel.
In the long run,
many mothers have lost their sons.
Placed in proper perspective,
worse things have happened.
In hindsight,
we had no choice.
Upon reflection,
we've never been a warlike people.
Biologically,
it's in our genes.
If you were in our shoes,
what would you have done?
Amazingly enough,
civilians often resemble tanks.
In geological terms,
this was just a blink in time.
Philosophically,
the truth is always relative.
Depending upon whom you believe,
it's all just a lie.
According to Darwin,
only the strong survive.
Strictly speaking,
who is my neighbor anyway?
In the words of Jesus,
suffer the little children.

From the National Center for Missing & Exploited Children

"Have you seen me?" they ask on the black-
and-white flyers that drift into my mailbox,
veinless leaves abandoned by the tree of light.

"Have you seen me?" in truck parks
late at night or loitering outside convenience stores
or floating face down on the shimmer

of a rainbowed ditch. "Have you seen me?"
Here he is in a photo taken at age five,
all gap-toothed innocence. Here she is,

the apple of some father's eye, her picture
aged to what she might have looked like at fifteen,
a girl missing more years than she was alive.

In a land that devours childhood, we hide them
in plain sight everywhere. They are nothing
now but the flicker of sun and shadow

when our cars click down the pavement,
the wind-torn voice that wakens us those nights
we can't remember who we are or where

we lie in darkness; the gray face staring at us
in the mirror each morning, flesh unnaturally aged,
a lost look haunting the furtive gaze.

The Fathers

Down in the basement, dead fathers move about,
bumping their heads on exposed beams,
trying without success to pick up tools
from the dusty workbench. If their words could reach us,
they'd ask for hot coffee and a smoke.
If their words could reach us they'd tell us how much
they regret having deployed the squadron of bombers
that drones overhead in our dreams every night.
They long to upgrade the circuit breaker,
replace the stained tile, paint the foundation red,
but all they can do is eye an empty pack
of cigarettes crumpled in the corner, then
go back to searching for the blueprints
to the family room that never got built.

Night Shift

Tonight your father returns to you as a woman,
death freeing him to face in two directions.
It's awkward for a little while:

his bony frame draped in crinoline,
his mouth shining beneath lip gloss, the long
silence he's endured making his voice rough,

pitched somewhere in the middle range,
like an old-fashioned clock on the verge of striking.
Now you can see the softness that was there all along

when he yielded to illness, in the maternal impulse
behind the years you've spent nurturing his memory.
If he picks you up bodily now as he used to do

when you were a boy, don't turn away.
Don't resist. Let him plant a fatherly kiss.
It's not just your dream anymore. It's also his.

Portrait of the Young Artist with Her Stepfather

He moves right in,
leaves his crusty toothbrush
on the bathroom sink.

Pats her head.
Calls her "Sweetheart."

Smiles behind his hand
when she's trying to play the piano.

Makes her mother laugh
a forced laugh.
God, she hates that.

Sometimes she catches him
looking at her.
Sometimes he catches her
looking at him.

Winks and jokes
that she better be careful
and not let any boy
trick her into swallowing
a watermelon.

At night, she tiptoes down the hall
and stands at the door to their bedroom
and watches the dark mountain
of his body looming
on the far side of her mother.

Someday
she's going to write about all this.

Grendel in the City

He's always run hot and this summer evening
finds him slumped in front of the open window
of his cramped second-story apartment, lights out,
dressed only in his underwear as he stares down
at the patrons spilling out of the pizza joint
just across the street, the voices coming to him
alien and unintelligible. "What kind of monster am I?"
he mutters to himself over and over. "What kind
of monster?" thinking of the girl he's lately pursued,
the girl who kept trying to flee, delicate and pale,
so beautiful that he could just devour her. And did.
Now with the off-shore breeze bringing no scent
of ocean, he belches a wet belch of regret,
scratches himself, and trudges off into the kitchen
to see what mother's dragged home for supper.

III.

Memorial Day Evening

Rustling, trees born
in another century
gather the day's mysteries
back into their crowns,
but even warm air,
rising from the earth,
cannot lift this weight.

An old picket fence sags—
gravity's nocked
bowstring. One by one,
streetlamps come on,
revealing some of the places
where you used to walk.

Danse Macabre

What I notice chiefly about the plastic skeleton
propped up inside a clear plastic dome on my son's dresser
is the extraordinary jauntiness, as if this collection
of ribs and vertebrae, skull bones and clavicle must figure
he has nothing left to lose. Left leg bent at the knee,
scalloped blade of his pelvis thrust forward, his arms,
as arranged by my boy, held in front of him, palms
facing out, elbows hyper-extended in an odd way,

he's like a man on a nearly abandoned dance floor
late at night beckoning to a shy woman to come
and join him in a jitterbug, all trace of vanity, all
self-consciousness about the spectacle he might be
making of himself fallen away so that he's left now
completely free to throw himself into life.

I marvel at the contrast between his loose-limbed
display and the state of my own skeleton, the click and
grind of worn-out joints, the ankle that no longer bends
to my will, the weight that permanently bears down
on my shoulders, the cranium knit together too tightly,
the jaw so burdened with worries that it is all I can do
to return his toothy invitation with a fleeting smile,
as though to say, "No thanks. I think I'll sit this one out."

Return to Eben Flood's Party

After Edward Arlington Robinson

Dusted with moonlight,
you stopped to toast yourself
up here where the winding
two-lane road turns and looks
back down on the valley.
In Tilbury Town, they'd
forgotten about the loneliness
that gnawed away at you,
the brother killed in a war
you were too young to fight in,
your wife driven mad
by the death of your only kid.
Years ago you fell and cracked
your skull open,
lying at home for a week
before anybody came looking,
but even now you still
haunt this place, with its
whiskey-scented damp
and mob of shadows.
So, here's to you, Mr. Flood.
I lift the jug and take a pull.
For want of love, or
something else you could
never quite put your finger on,
you gathered by yourself
on a night just like this.
You drank alone.

Neanderthal Burial Site

How keenly they must have felt the loss,
they who were so few, they who spent
their days peering off into the distances,
at herds of animals that vastly
outnumbered them, the sky reminding
them every day they were small
and they were alone. Eyes turned inward,
facing each other across the circle,
maybe they had no name for this.
Maybe they had no names for anything,
just ready-made customs, like the one
where they folded the arms and legs
so that the body cradled itself, or the gesture
they made with the hand, breaking
a flower stem just beneath the blossom
as a way of signifying wordless pain.

Voice from Lascaux

I was angry
until I realized I was one of them,
stick figures sprung from barren ground,
my hands clumsier than stone,
the cut above my brow
bleeding into their eyes.

In these, the earliest attempt
to explain ourselves,
we are always lying on our backs,
limbs stiff with awe, not crawling,
trying to remember
how to walk on all fours.

Only the beasts floating overhead
are fully-imagined,
three-dimensional, flesh-colored,

still hunting us down.

A Russian Sailor Recalls Dying on The *Kursk*

Near the end, in the dark and utter cold, the hearts
of some us grew buoyant, rising like bubbles
to bump against the frozen bulkhead. Outside
the groans of deep sea pressure became the song
of wood spirits flitting in and out of birch groves
back home and the icy grate beneath our feet
sprang up as sun-warmed rye grass between bare toes.
And then, one by one, as we slipped out the front
of the ruined hull and met the Arctic's weight,
our souls divided into a higher and lower order,
part floating upward toward shafts of moted light,
the rest sinking to the ocean floor where they
joined the slow pelagic current, circling the globe,
staining the black waters like a cloud of ink.

Life Itself

Solitary figures lumbering across a winter scene—
how they seem to embody (or, better yet, disembody)
the loneliness, the isolation, the melancholy edge
of this kind of day. Distant even when drawing near,
yearning for human contact despite having buried
the tenderest parts of themselves beneath bundles

of wool clothes. They're like the late afternoon sun,
pale and fitful, drifting in and out of focus like images
in a feverish dream. You can almost hear them asking,
"What, except life itself, can we call a fateful opportunity
we have no choice but to accept or reject?" You'd reach out,
try to offer them what scant solace you might command,

but draw back like the early-rising moon that appears
but soon retreats behind a cloud. They remind you
too much, these figures, of that old bachelor uncle who,
even like tonight's moon, used to smile down on you wanly
as he dispensed the sum of wisdom he thought he'd
earned living out his existence in the echoing back wards

of a now-abandoned asylum for the hopelessly insane.

The Dead of Winter

We speak of this time
as though it were a place,
a battlefield strewn
with corpses,
a burial ground
of shattered statues
hooded with snow.
And we picture
something grainy, gray-
and-white, crow-like figures
hunching inside capes,
frost working its claw
into the heart of trees.
In this zone we hear
an echo, a dread voice
that chills words to zero.
Over on the dark shore
branches snap like bones.
Scurrying across the ice,
we wait for the crack,
never looking down
into the depths, so close
but a lifetime away,
the final holding tank
of those we couldn't
hope to save.

Upon Receiving My Brother's Ashes

Good-bye, brother. And hello. Our childhood
died with you in that sealed Florida room
where you exiled yourself, the shades
drawn, your swollen heart burst at last,
nothing in the refrigerator, the TV on.
Now there's no one to ask
the name of the neighbor boy's cousin
who fell through the ice on Mirror Lake
and drowned, or of the candy store
out on the highway, or where we were the day
we drank homemade root beer, then played
pirate ship with other kids in a dusty barn.
All I have of you now is this bronze box
filled with ashes (not even a proper urn),
the sweepings of your life. What would I
find if I pried open its seal and peeked inside?
Some powdery substance, gritty and fine,
like the beach we used to play on, the sand
so hot in the mid-day sun that even
in the time it took us to run to the lake
the soles of our feet would burn.

Hydrangeas

It was at your grandma's house where
you first became acquainted with hydrangeas,
how the rain would bend them over
but then, when the skies cleared
and the wind stopped blowing, how they'd
recover their upright posture again
until that one big rain would come
when the days were growing shorter
and fall-like weather had set in and leave them
bowed down for good this time, a gathering
of white-haired ladies burdened, as was
your grandma, with memories of the dead.

My Mother's Japanned Jewelry Box

The lacquered shell still looks wet,
a reminder that even wood is
a kind of liquid, the grain
running now wavy, now straight,
the current of electrons holding
steady, but only for a moment,
in my hands, which are also
flowing, as all things flow away.

And beneath an inky jet-black lid
that gleams like the night sky
out over water, the rings and
necklaces and semi-precious gems
she left behind, thinking she'd
soon be back, glisten,
waiting to be fingered again
like pebbles at the bottom of a stream.

August Sunset from the Highest Point in St. Paul

How we'd like to hope that our lives, too,
will turn to gold just before they set,
the all-too-familiar silhouette of the city
backlit, burnished, with a refulgent glow
beneath a slowly-developing, redemptive
vision of the earth's rim lifting to meet
a sky flushed with rose-colored flame,
and then, as darkness finally settles in,
lights coming on in the river valley far below.

In the Winter Garden of Stillborn Babies

This is where we hoped they'd arrive:
the children who did not flower, flower here.
The air is humid, womb-like,
the way they would have liked it
if they'd ever woke to liking,
slowly stirred by the overhead fan
that turns with the whir and hum
of blood pumping through veins.
The soil in these planting beds is rich,
undepleted, and the stems that bud
but do not bloom glow from within
like a hand cupped around a flame.
An eyeless statue of St. Francis watches
over them, arms extended downward
as a sign he won't abandon them,
he will never return to heaven,
he will remain here where they lay,
sleeping at his feet, undisturbed,
his little flock of flightless birds.

Sorrow Personified

Sorrow, old-fashioned gal,
you've passed your life alone,
from maiden- into matronhood,
wearing my mother's cast-off
expressions, your Doric gown,
arms grown heavy with the years.
Now no one seeks you anymore,
there in the sheltered grove,
thick with verdigris.

Still, you shine for me sometimes
on grief's abandoned altars,
not in darkness like the stars
(compression leads to fixity,
and ice is the death of tears),
but in the shadows at the end
of an ever-closing day,
when all of autumn's muted colors
glow beneath the clouds.

Listening to a CD of Glenn Gould Performing "The Goldberg Variations"

You can hear him in the background
if you listen closely, his voice a little hoarse
and off-key, creating its own counterpoint.
Faint at first, the crackling sound builds
as his fingers dig deep into the score,
swelling in the slower movements, fading
in the fast, though never disappearing.
Strange how he felt compelled to add
his own wordless singing to the track,
even if it meant marring the perfection
of his performance, or maybe *because*
it meant marring that perfection,
as if over the years every time he sat down
at a keyboard he found it harder and harder
not to notice how much a grand piano resembles
a coffin, the lid propped open to reveal
steel tendons and felt-covered knucklebones.
And so he sang, and still sings, heartfelt
if out of tune, his spirit living on in the spaces
between the notes, where we all live,
stepping lightly up and down the staff,
leaping nervously over every pause, never
more than one full-stop away from silence.

Inertia

The little towns we hurry though
on our way to some place bigger?
Almost empty now.
The streets and rundown shops—
no one's about.
The pioneer church is abandoned.
So is the one-room schoolhouse.
If you glimpse a light in a window
near the top of a hill,
that's probably someone
sitting up there all alone.

In general
it's only the cemetery that's full,
as if to illustrate some law or rule
about how movement,
seeking its own level,
goes underground

before coming back as stone.

On the Highway to Heaven

Out here, fiery wrecks
are restored,
overturned LP tanker trucks
blaze with a flame that
burns but does not consume,

the twisted hulks of loaded
station wagons
carrying families
to the vacations they will never
return from are righted,
back in lane,

father behind the wheel
permanently stalled
in that happy moment
just before the crash
when his eye was caught
by his son pointing out
the hawk forever lifting off
from a fencepost.

And here the sleepy travelers
wake in time,
this time,
to pull their cars back
across the center line

and drunks
crawl out from smoking heaps,
grin crookedly and ask
for another drink,

and all the girls who ever
disappeared
hitchhiking home from college
stand beside the road,
resurrected in their youth,
innocent thumbs

stuck out again.

Twilight

The west-facing room
deepens into darkness
and, gradually, I disappear.
Sounds of breathing.
Who's there?

Whatever your name,
you that join me now,
stay by my side.
Wake me gently
when it's time to go.
Lead me by the hand
toward the morning star.

IV.

Stop and Go

Every time you end up
waiting at the one stoplight
in some small Midwestern town,
you think you should pick up some flowers
and drop them off with the residents.
You know what it feels like to be abandoned,
how isolation isn't just loneliness
but the breeding ground of chaos,
how memories, unchecked,
can turn around and consume their host.

But then you think about the catch
in the throat of some old woman
when it's time to leave,
the offer of one more cup of coffee,
the invitation to stay for dinner,
the desperate plea that you wait
just a little bit longer until the lemon bars
cool off enough to be eaten.
There's only one merciful thing to do.
When the light turns green,

you keep on going.

The Work of Silos

How sad the silos look these summer
evenings, sunset painting their steel walls
livid from the bottom to the top,

their shadows reaching out to harvest the rise
of darkness. Cleats set into a drifting sky,
they have held the land in place all day.

Here, the restless fields of corn, gathered
into shocks, are stopped and stored away.
Here the outward flow of life tips back

to fulfill another year's containment.
Yet tonight, beneath a weathered moon,
its leading edge worn smooth as by a current,

these same silos will serve as a pivot point
around which dreams will wheel when they
return to us from beyond the place

where the stars all drown in morning light.

In Exile

What secrets are they sharing,
the sparrows in the barren trees?
All morning they fatten themselves
on the thin syrup of winter light.

Over the hum of the space heater
I listen to their chatter, smiling distractedly.
I am like a refugee, newly arrived
in a land whose melodious tongue
I might understand some day
although never hope to master.

When We Are Gone

What will the creek sound like when we are gone?
Will the trees no longer be bowed down
when the metaphors we impose on them fall to the ground?
Will the birds hop as skittishly when we are not?
Or will they move about with a less spasmodic gait?
For whom will the squirrel celebrate
after finding a safe perch no hand can reach?
How will the world manage when we've fled the scene?
From this little clearing, I step back a pace
and watch sunlight fill the vacated space.

Dream World

Amazing all the things that hide in sleep—
alien worlds, foreign cities,
streets you roamed as a kid,
streets you walked on in love or in pain.

From where does this river
with all its beautiful debris rise,
before sweeping past and littering
its banks with dreams?

And now, here comes the father
you never had a chance to know as a man,
stepping forth out of the shadows
to ask if you'd like to join him in a drink.

Try to understand.
All of life is about separation.
Darkness giving birth to light.
Light dying into darkness,
love a wrench missing
from somebody's ribcage.

Maybe that's why when
we're finally linked two-by-two,
we're so willing to walk up
the gangplank together,

our eyes on the clouds that
will lower the shutter
on all the bright
but painful differences,
drowning them in an indivisible flood

of murky water.

Back Door Man

I found the back door to the world today.
It's small, hardly visible from a distance,
haloed by leaves,
but up close enormous—
big enough to march an army through.

On the other side, you see a lot things
you'd never see coming,
like the way people look at you
when they think you aren't looking
and what they say about each other
if they think nobody's listening.

But, there's other things, too,
like young boys playing with a ball
as if it were 1954
and a frozen sea of golden rye
and a night sky that shines as bright as noon
and a clear vision of what lies ahead
lying behind your eyes

and a whole different way of keeping time
where you wake tomorrow
and it's yesterday morning
and just when you think everything's done
you discover the end is just the beginning

and you've barely even begun.

The Bookish Life

There have been times in my life
when books have meant as much or more
to me than people. When, exhausted
by the tribulations of a social order that
can seem devoid of beauty, truth or logic,
a book of ancient history or an analysis
of the mythology of some far off place
or a collection of Spanish poems
keeping time around a gypsy fire
have opened the arms of their pages
and welcomed me into their embrace.

Friends, if you yourselves would like
to mean as much to me, try approaching
in a bookish fashion, which is not to say
narrow and pedantic, but in a way
likely to inspire an expansive reading,
full of dog-eared passages that I
crave returning to again and again.

Sundays Spent Working at Home

It always make me feel so virtuous,
as if this were not my own, but God's house,
the words on the page falling bright and dense,
the snow outside a rite of innocence

renewed. Holy this hour. Holy the groan
of wind and walls, the child's voice in the next room,
the walk we'll take a little later with the dog
beside the river and around the bog.

And holy the still-later, winding-down time
with a book in the bath, a glass of wine
and a mind that continues to spark
long after I lie down and pray to the dark.

The Day After

Today is always the day after
and the day before the day
when all of yesterday's disorder
has gotten a little worse
but not as bad as it will be tomorrow
when everything will be the same
as now, only a little more so.
Today is the day when the weather
has taken a turn for the worse
or a turn for the better
or is pretty much unchanged,
depending on the weather.

Today is the day you're thinking
of moving to a place where
the weather's better or where
you'd be closer to family or,
depending on your family,
a little further away from that band
of neurotic bloodsuckers.
Today is the day that yesterday
you did or didn't put things off to
and the day when you will or won't
put things off until tomorrow,

which may or may not come,
a subject that's certainly worth
thinking about but maybe
at another time, like tomorrow,
so let's put that off lest we spoil
our ability to enjoy ourselves today,
a day that will never come again,
unless of course it does,
but then that's what you might call

a story for another day.

As Long as Possible

Morning light not caught between
day or night but instead uncertain
whether it wants to grow up at all
to become another afternoon troubled,

as so often happens, by stormy arguments
and a sticky haze rising from Earth's
body heat and ending with a decline
into a feeble state in which it might
even be unable to remember if it fell
today or yesterday or the day before.

Let's hope there's plenty of time left
to brew a cup of tea and make some toast.
Enough time to settle back
and invite the morning light to stay

just like it is now, as long as possible.

The Thunderhead Speaks

We gather our dark forces,
tall faces glowering.

Jagged blades
flash in our pockets.
We knock the wind
sprawling before us.

Far below we see books
lying open everywhere.

Let the pages
assigned to record your stories
try to flee.

They will be liquidated.

Evening Clouds

There are days when I, too,
want to lift myself aloft like them,
visible everywhere,
but still alone,
vapor piled up
into a deep sorrowing tower
harboring pockets of shadow
almost hidden from the sun—
See how sad you've made me!
But then the wind that always blows
across my life picks up,
feathery breaths rise
into the current circulating the globe,
and I move on,
into another night, another day,
never holding still in the luminous
dark places, raining myself empty
into the ground.

Weather Report

Those rainy days when I was a kid?
Let me explain. I hadn't yet developed
a grown-up's taste for having time
on my hands. I'd sit in my bedroom,
feeling bored and restless, and listen
to the drumbeat on the roof, the rhythm
turning from fast to slow then back again.

And in doing so, I'd fall into a reverie
(though I had no word for it then)
and would end up feeling that *I* was the rain
as well as the voices I could hear
talking among themselves in the rain,
and the variations on shades of gray
between clouds that hung low and others
that seemed to hang a little higher,
and my heart would skip and flutter
in those brief moments of clearing
when sun gave way to shadow and
then shadow gave way to sun
like somebody opening and closing
a shutter in quick succession.

Yes, just thinking about it can
take me right back to those
rainy days. So if you come upon me
and I seem deep in thought, please
do me a favor and keep moving on.
No matter what the weather outside,
I may be listening to the rain.

The Tall Wind

The tall wind is blowing today.
Nothing can stop it. It's deep enough
to drown the treetops, shallow enough
to ripple across the lawn, a river of grass
like the Everglades. It reaches up
to pull down sparrows
from the sky, then leans over
to look at its face in every puddle
or backyard birdbath. Why does
it come? To test the moving parts
of shrubs and flowers? To make
the gate hinge squeak to remind us
it needs an oiling? To separate
the dead branches from the living
in the blighted elm? To peel loose shingles
from the roof, a kind of confetti?
Like joy, like sorrow, it makes us
turn away quickly, water filling our eyes.
And though empty and invisible,
like the thing we mean when we say
"life," just look how the tall wind
bends us all beneath its weight.

The Snow

It's almost my oldest habit of all,
watching the snow fall in thick
white ropes that hiss as they uncoil,
or that studiously frost the dark peaks

of spruce, or that, on days like this,
come down as thin flakes, sparsely spaced,
wavering rhythmically on the breeze
before turning into tearstreaks

when they touch the windshield, the year's
accumulated burden of frozen grief—
the wars, the dangers, the deaths—
thawing on contact.

And let me not forget a snowfall's
restorative effects: how it brings me
wide awake when I'm drowsy
or can bestow a measure of peace

if I'm tense, or turn me instantly
into a child again when I'm feeling old.
I climb out of the car and stretch
my arms as wide as I can.

Snowflakes touch my ungloved palms
with fingertips that are delicate
and chill (Cold hands, warm heart!).
We dance.

On Moss

Blesséd be the moss that beards the face
of exposed embankments deep in the forest,

that spreads a feathery caul over old stones,
breaking them down, starting them on their way

from loneliness toward the community of soil.
And blesséd be the moss that lays its carpet across

the north-facing toes of white birch trees, showing
the direction down paths it will never follow.

And blesséd be the moss that comforts
the torn hoof of the starving doe in winter,

and that waits patiently beneath
ice-crusted, knee-deep late January snow,

to keep for us, who might otherwise despair,
the jewel-green promise of our renewal.

Every River

A meadow gone soggy underfoot.
Crops damaged by a hailstorm.
A desert in bloom.
A child swept away by the current.

Every river is a reminder
of cause-and-effect,
a record of what happened
at a distance,
in the past,
somewhere out of sight.

Whose heart has thawed.

Whose heart remains
locked in winter.

Lunar Eclipse

February 20, 2008

The moon looks
stunned, like a patient
going under,

but in truth
it is only drowning,
always drowning

beneath the tide
it sends running
from pole to pole.

Here on Earth's slowly
advancing prow,
we watch

our umbra submerge
the bright disk
in a rusty glow

like bog water leaching
iron from the soil.
Curious how

the hard winter sky
seems to soften now
until it becomes

almost welcoming,
a landscape to be
ventured across,

our feet sinking
with every step,
but our faces raised

toward a vision
of heaven that,
for once,

we all can share.

Deep in Outer Space

They could tune into our old broadcasts,
hear Hitler denounce Churchill
for the first time again,
or watch Jack Benny do a slow burn,
or listen to him play the violin
with a noise a meteorite might make
scratching against an asteroid
if there were any sound
in the perfect vacuum of space.

Or they could train a telescope our way
and see the dust clouds rise
from the huge herds of buffalo and black rhino,
or a strange elliptical shadow
passing across the face of the Great Plains
as a flock of Passenger Pigeons comes between
earth and the sun.

Or they could read by the glow
of our vanished cities,
or puzzle over the fires
erupting all around the world
just before we blinked out
like an old star.

And if they are attentive,
someday they could even replay
our most recent day before yesterday,
or observe your mother weeding
in the garden in the final hour
before her collapse,
or hear all the words
leading up to the final words
that tear the couple apart
and bear their love swiftly
out into the darkness

like light fleeing its source.

The Sunflowers

Whoever named them must have known
what has only lately been revealed
by telescopes and computer simulations:
the mass of petals arranged like solar flares
around a honeycombed interior,
the seed row swirling outward in a ratio
shared by both the Milky Way and the chambers
of a conch shell. Standing in a field,
they reveal the unsettling truth that the sun
we have always believed to be unique and ours alone
is only one of countless other stars,
each pulsating, each shedding light on a swarm
of planets circling like bees, a vision
of the cosmos in which everything is
one and yet, like us, infinitely various.

Peonies

Still buds, but on the verge of blooming,
    they bow toward the west,
        driven by lust for the arc
           of the afternoon sun.

Taut as cocked guns,
    they lean far out over their stems,
        racers near the finish line,
           straining to breast the tape.

But victory will be ours,
    not theirs, in the moment
        when they spill their scent
           like milt released into a freshet

to swim upstream through
    the bedroom window where it finds us
        panting, side by side, in a blossom
        of rose-colored sheets.

Spendthrifts

How easily new love
turns us into spendthrifts!
Day and night,
we squander the hours
as if we owned them.

2.

Your heart beats beneath my ear.
My ear drums against your chest.
Summer gives birth to summer,
springtime is on the dessert menu.
Each season curls up
inside every other season.

Now my mouth drifts
toward your bare breast.
In unison almost

we shiver.

3.

You thought you
were just helping
to set her free
but ended up
knocking down the cage
you didn't even know
you were trapped inside.

Turns out, touching
her sandy bottom
was just the first step
toward sounding

your own depths.

4.

She's a pool
with no shallow end.

No wonder you keep
jumping in!

5.

We arrive again at the solstice
only on different ends of world.
I am here, but we are gone,
separate as night and day,
married like dusk and dawn.
There can be no joining together,
not really, unless we are free
to come and go.

Did you see how I fell to my knees
without even noticing it?
Steel and glass and a wary heart
cannot protect us, but sunlight
arranges the valley floor into a puzzle
of bright and shadowy pieces.

Don't be fooled
by the tomcat's stillness.
He has the mid-day heat
trapped beneath his paws.

Cote de Valais

after Rilke's French poems

Take heed of how these mountain freshets,
spilling into the stone-dressed drains
that bear them through the village,
go on making their own weather,
thick clouds here, a deep blue sky elsewhere,
waking each rock they touch, turning
every obstacle into a fountain of song.
And if a small current happens to wander
into a side-channel, her sisters
come quickly to take her by the hand
and send her tumbling again downhill,
crying out, 'Hurry along now! There are
flowerbeds thirsting in the valley!
Young brides waiting to be quickened
by a shower of pearls!

Between the Covers

The books I left out in the backyard last night
are swollen this morning with dew,
loaves of raw dough leavened by starlight,
the lungs of asthmatic children
breathing deeply at summer camp.
The fresh air has done them good.
Calmed by contact with nature,
they speak more slowly now,
the interval between their words
a little longer than before.

I pick them up and bring them inside.
They have witnessed how the moon
starves herself each month
in a nervous bid for attention.
They know by the thoughtful way I turn them over
and run my fingers across their pages
that they are valued for their inner worth,
for their depth and even their flaws,
like a beloved wife grown
fat and beautiful over the years.

This Isn't a Dream?

Is it all right to have a happy memory about donuts?

Is it possible for me to reopen one of the small service windows
at Horn & Hardart's and retrieve a slice of apple pie?

Is it okay to recall a night in December when I was 12 and snow
was falling heavy and straight down and hissing like rain
and I passed a kid I didn't even know going the other direction
and we both said, "Merry Christmas" to each other?

Are there any objections if one of the things I remember most clearly
about my father are his hands, how they were almost square
and that when he opened them the fingers splayed out
like the delta of some powerful and mysterious river?

Would anyone mind if I admit that I've reached a point
where I want to stop striving all the time and just let life
flow over me like the incoming tide of a warm ocean current?

And is it acceptable if my love for you and your love for me
isn't a prairie fire (though one could flare up at any time!)
but more like a quiet house that we've built together and

filled with comfortable furniture, a place where I can fall asleep
holding your hand and wake up in the night and see you
lying beside me and realize "This isn't a dream. This is real"?

The Fishmonger's Wife

Evenings he comes home smelling
of those parts of the sea that cannot escape,
entangled in old nets, thrashing
and moaning as it tries to break free.
She met him when she was the girl
behind the counter who kept
the pier-side café open late
so he could come and eat,
their banter tart as lemon juice.
Now they eat chowder and fishcakes,
the same silence every night.
In bed, he becomes the back slope
of a nor'easter, breathing the names
of storms and shipwreck shoals
while she lies beside him, rocking
in his wake, waiting for the tide
to come in and sweep her away.

Everyday Low Prices

This romance is like
a discount department store.
It's got everything you want
but nothing you really need.
Bobble-head statues, water rifles,
marked-down DVD's,
lots of stuff with beads
with no purpose at all
except gathering dust
or tripping you up
if they fall on the floor.

But no nails or first-aid kits
or stapling guns or twine or tape
or glue to patch things up
when they're falling apart.
No legal pads for jotting down
what we've begun to forget.
No aspirin, no antacid,
no cough medicine
to help you stop clearing
your throat when I talk,
no herb supplements
to relieve a heavy heart,
no hammers, no bolts,
no screwdrivers, not even
a set of cables to jump start
an old engine that refuses

to turn over in the morning.

Song of the Fat Woman Swimming off Cocoa Beach

I come here every chance I get.
The ocean always wants me,
always takes me in its arms.
When it lifts me, I grow buoyant.
My edges dissolve with each salt lick.

Now I'm a first-time mother again,
lulling my newborn to sleep
to the sound of the waves,

now a teenager sunbathing
with my friends,

now a chubby toddler,
wading naked in the surf,
too caught up in play
to hear my own mother calling me:

"Come away from the water now!
It's time to eat!"

Anatomy Lesson

1.

This is my arm
paused between
a forelimb and a wing.
These are my hands,
neither fins
nor a spiderweb of stars.
This is my blood
smiling in my kidneys,
this my heart
hammering out borrowed time.
This is my skull
where warm oceans lap,
giving birth to electrons.
These are my eyes
where everything I see
floats by two-by-two.
These are my ribs
where my chest hangs out,
This is my navel
like a record of the winter kill.
These are my legs,
a fork in the lightning,
and these are my feet,
two boney kids
who finally grew up
and carried me to you.

2.

At this moment,
my hand on the small of your back.
my leg lying across yours.

At this moment,
your thigh and the slow moon rise
of your pelvis
cresting my horizon line.

At this moment,
my fingers trickling down the rill of your spine.
At this moment
your eyes, your hair, the faint luster
of your shoulder.

At this moment,
your smile, your lips lifting to meet mine.
At this moment,
the earth turning over, the garden,
the bud, the flower, the fragrance,
the evening hour.

At this moment,
before the moment
just after the moment
when moments paused
for a moment,
at this moment
before all the moments

still to come.

The Shining

There's a lot to be said about light
and almost nothing that
can be written without it.
It pours into the room this morning
and guides your pen across the paper.
It draws you to the window and whispers,
"Open your eyes and see!"

And now it flows across the bed
and takes on the shape of your love.
Rising on her elbow, she smiles,
her eyes gleaming as if to say,

"Slide over here now.
 Shine on me."

Some Mornings

Rain on the roof,
a sudden downpour
that floods the gutters,

and gushes over the eaves,
flattening the grass,
washing away the childhood
bruises you felt again last night.

Some mornings the gray light says
it's okay to go outside
looking like this.

V.

Autumn Tutorial

Summer's over.
The trees shed their leaves.
The days grow brighter
even as they get shorter;
so much sky was hidden
behind that shade.
Is this how you want me
to come to you, Lord—
self-disarmed, a broken
pane of glass through which
light and air both stream?
Is that why I've noticed
the less I speak the more
you seem inclined to listen?

Rain Dance

The rain today comes unbidden
as it always does,
an endless sequence of notes
from the oldest music
ever composed.
I see it peck the dust
with one-toed prints.
I feel it fall on me from above,
furling dark wings
on my shoulders,
eyeing the watery elements
it plans to carry off some day,
rain that returns
our sulfur dioxide,
our strontium-90,
the ash and soot of buildings
we've set ablaze,
the cities we turn
into clouds of smoke,
all come back to us,
the sacrifice of Cain
refused once more,
rain that leaves a dry outline
beneath my feet
like the rim of a hole
dug in the ground,
that marks the path
when I finally move,
rain that lifts from the trees
like a flock of invisible birds,
that fishes the river,
that glistens like a blade
on the turning whetstone,
rain that whispers and whispers
this mild spring day
in a disembodied voice
that makes me shiver.

The Stone Arch Bridge

Minneapolis, Minnesota

It's been here a century or more,
proof that whenever you cross water
you end up spanning time as well.
Like hand-made arches everywhere
it doesn't derive its strength solely
from resistance but from the way
each rough-cut stone leans
against another, the burden
shared by all, the force of gravity
thrust back into the earth like a taproot
seeking nourishment from the soil.
Kinetic energy fixed in place
this way translates into solid form,
beauty fused to usefulness, function
inseparable from form: The dome
of a stone shelter to keep us dry and warm.
The footings of a bridge that we
might cross to embrace each other.

It's the blue everyone is talking about

from a line by Frank O'Hara

It's the blue everyone is talking about,
authentic, bold, humble, interrogatory,
so different now that it's been pointed out
from the aqua-green everyone was talking about
yesterday, anticipating in its cunning use
of harmonics and half-tones that appear
to hover on the edge of visible light the color
everyone will be talking about tomorrow,
although we must admit, now you mention it,
to feeling a bit ashen over the possibility
that someone may already be talking
about that next big color and we don't even
know what it is yet. But anyway, everyone talking
and trying hard to look as if we are listening
about the blue that comes as a welcome relief
from the aqua-green that seemed to be everywhere
yesterday, in the lofts that, in retrospect
now look a little too spare, a little too eager
to make a statement, and all the while
some kind of colorless vapor filling up
the spaces inside, making us a little edgy,
until someone drops a glass on the floor
and we jump, startled by the explosion
of shards and then we laugh and joke about
a narrow escape as the hostess hurries in
to clean up and the young woman who dropped
the glass—no one seems to know who she is—
lowers her eyes and turns crimson.

The French Language Tapes

By the end of tape 4-B I'm ready to kill them:
Madame Durand and Monsieur Lelong
trying to decide where and at what time
to have lunch; Janine, the young woman
who will not fail to pass along M. Durand's
good wishes to her parents, still vacationing,
still vacationing, not in Paris but in Lyon,
accompanied by the brother from whom

Janine has had no news; the clerk at the hotel
in Montmartre who has a very nice room
on the first floor; the chamber maid
who'll not only show the guest his room
but transport his baggage for him;
and the mysterious guest himself, checking in
alone though his family will be joining him
in a few days (and what will he be doing

in the meantime? Enjoying, perhaps,
a secret assignation with Janine, out from
under the watchful eye of her parents
who are still vacationing, still vacationing
in Lyon, and not in Paris?), all of them
speaking very slowly, repeating everything,
enunciating each word as if all they want
is to hear themselves talk. As I listen

I think of the mental game I used to play
with myself when I was a child, saying
a word over and over in my head
until its meaning separated from its sound
like the soul leaving the body's alphabet.
And then I remember the argument
I once witnessed in Spain, pitting
a janitor against the manager of a dorm

at the University of Madrid, the manager
angrily demanding *"Porque?"*, the janitor
shrugging, answering "Porque no?" back
and forth, back and forth, *"Porque?!"* "Porque no?"
"Why?!" "Why not?" *"Why?!"* "Why not?"
like a dialogue between two madmen
on an instruction tape showing you how
to drive someone crazy in any language.

Salud y Dinero

This bag of salad greens doesn't taste
like 12 hours of back-breaking work
in direct summer sun with no trace of shade,
or of the permanent squint you wear
when sweat drips down your face
and you don't get the chance to wipe it away
because it'll put you behind on your schedule
and you've got to meet your quota because
grandma's sick again and little Rosa's
running a fever and even the free clinic
costs you money.
And it doesn't taste of aching knees, either,
or 15 minute breaks two times a day, or the beans
and tortillas getting soggy in a lunch bucket
or of rocking back and forth on your feet
as you try to forget you need to pee
and swollen feet and a straw boss
cheating you out of nickels and dimes
at the of the week (Who broke the handle
on that basket? You know how much
those clippers cost, Jose?!)
No, it doesn't taste of any of these,
nor the smell of being on the run
and your heart stopping every time
ICE cruisers pull up next to the field
or the longing you feel for the friends
who got sent back and the guilt
over having ducked in time
when they came to round people up
on the bus with bars in its windows.
No, it doesn't taste or smell
of any of these things, but they're
all there, wrapped up in every bite,
so, eat up, amigos. Salud y dinero
(especially dinero!) y tiempo para gustarlos!

Jesus of Walmart

They liked the radiant smile, his upbeat manner
and so, despite a scanty work record—
"Assistant carpenter, then three years
wandering the hills"—they hired him
as a greeter, the wages from his full-time,
28-hour-a-week job not enough to cover
the company's health insurance. "Get sick
around here and you just have to heal yourself,"
muttered a disgruntled "associate," a 50-ish mother
whose crippled daughter got up the very
next day and walked, everybody calling it
a miracle, just like that special order
of tee-shirts that sold for $1.99 each.
Now he wanders the aisles in a pair
of plastic sandals made in China,
reminding shoppers of special savings
they'll find if they only keep on searching,
pointing out the counter where
you can redeem coupons clipped from
somebody's discarded newspaper,
consoling the single moms when they
discover food-stamps can't be used
to buy the sugary cereal their fatherless
kids clamor for each morning. In aisles
lined with desolate frowns he smiles,
asking weary late-night shoppers if he
can help, talking softly, respectfully
to those who have never known anything
but contempt and the presumption
of guilt. To the illegals sneaking in
after a hard day of underpaid work,
men named Jose, woman called Maria,
he speaks in tongues they haven't heard
since leaving home in search of plenty.

The lonely, the desperate, the stoned,
those who've given up hope, he steers
ever-so-gently away from Hardware
with its brackets of nails and coils
of rope. Look at me, he says.
I have no home, no place to rest
my head. But even on a Saturday night
when it's raining outside, and the last
bus left 15 minutes ago, there is a place
that's always open, offering light,
offering the chance that when the price
of going on even another day seems
beyond reach, you'll find what you need
and it will cost you little, it will cost you
nothing. Just heed my words,
he urges everyone. Have a little faith.

Dark Day

Dark day that doesn't brighten past dawn,
all your hours are waking hours.
I love your soft breath, your quiet voice,
your palate of subdued colors.
Teach me the spirit of watchful waiting.
Rouse my every moment from its sleep.

Acknowledgments

Some of the poems in *Jesus of Walmart* have appeared in the following publications

Journals

Art Word Quarterly: "A Russian Sailor Recalls Dying on the
  Kursk"
Atlanta Review: "Swimming Laps"
Eclipse: "Between the Covers," "From the National Center
  for Missing & Exploited Children" "My Grandfather
  at Rest"
Fifth Column: "This Endless Night"
Green Blade: "Hardly Paradise," "Rain Dance"
Into the Teeth of the Wind: "Photograph of the Students in the
  One-Room Finnish Schoolhouse, Elko, Minnesota,
  1914," "Sorrow Personified"
Lief: section #2 of "Anatomy Lesson," sections #2-5,
  "Spendthrifts"
New York Quarterly: "As Long as Possible," "Weather Report"
Notre Dame Review: "North of San Diego"
Permafrost: "Neanderthal Burial Site"
Poetry East: "The Fathers," "Evening Clouds," "Sorrow
  Personified," "Autumn Tutorial," "Between the
  Covers," "Dark Day," "Sunflowers," "Spendthrifts"
North Dakota Quarterly: "On the Highway to Heaven"
Out of Line: "At the Auto Junkyard," "Imperial Lexicon,"
  "The Stone Arch Bridge"
Permafrost: "Neanderthal Burial Site"
Rhino: "Night Shift"
Slant: "Peonies" "Voice from Lascaux"
Talking River Review: "My Mother's Japanned Jewelry Box"
Turtle Island Quarterly: "Stop and Go," "For Local Poets
  Everywhere," "Portrait of the Young Artists with Her
  Stepfather"
Turtle Quarterly: "The Fishmonger's Wife" "Listening to a CD
  of Glenn Gould Performing 'The Goldberg
  Variations'"

Anthologies

Tzimtzum (Mercury Heartlink, 2013): "Jesus of Walmart."
"The Long Drive Down," "Autumn Tutorial,"
"Between the Covers," "Swimming Laps," "All
Present and Accounted For," "Cote de Valais,"
"Boys Fishing," "August Sunset from the Highest
Point in St. Paul," "On the Highway to Heaven,"
"Song of the Fat Woman off Cocoa Beach," "The
Boxing Lesson," "Upon Receiving My Brother's
Ashes," "Dark Day," "Every River," "Listening to a CD
of Glenn Gould Performing 'The Goldberg
Variations'"

Perfect in their Art: Poems about Boxing (University of Southern
Illinois Press, 2003): "The Boxing Lesson"

Chapbooks

Rain Dance, (Parallel Press, University of Wisconsin, 2011):
"The Fishmonger's Wife," "Imperial Lexicon,"
"At the Auto Junkyard," "Neanderthal Burial Site,"
"Rain Dance," "The Snow," "The Fathers," "The
Stone Arch Bridge," "From the National Center
for Missing & Exploited Children," "This Endless
Night," "Hardly Paradise," "A Russian Sailor Recalls
Dying on The *Kursk*"

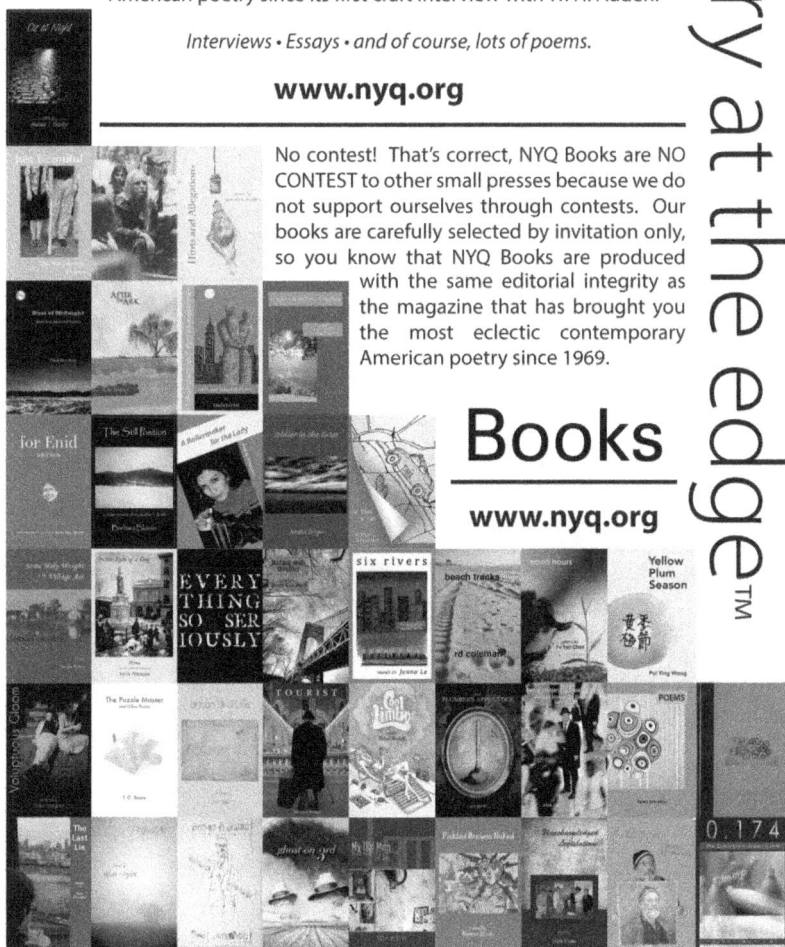

www.ingramcontent.com/pod-product-compliance
Lightning Source LLC
LaVergne TN
LVHW091225080426
835509LV00009B/1167